the
100-Day Self-Discovery Journal

Breakthrough Journal Writing Prompts for Self-Exploration,
Direction and Improving Your Life

Written by Mackenzie Reed
Created by Journal Mastery

Dedication

This journal is dedicated to all the souls wishing to discover themselves and changing for a life different to the one they currently lead.
Welcome to the beginning of a new journey!

Table of Contents

Introduction

Congratulations and thank you for joining me and other likeminded journal fellows on the amazing self-discovering journal journey!

In this book, I present to you my favorite journal writing prompts specifically for getting to know yourself, what you want, and how to be a more authentic you. I envision these prompts will help you take your journaling to a new level of challenging and exciting self-discovery as they have done for me. I'm confident the prompts will help you get new insights and bring a different perspective with results and outcomes that go far beyond journaling.

How to use the Journal

The 100-Day Self-Discovery Journal is simple to use. First, decide if you want to write in this book or purchase a notebook of your choice. Alternatively, if you prefer to work on a computer or laptop, set up a Word document. Second, think about when you would like to complete your journal entries. Though some people may fill them in at any time of the day, for a real surge of inspiration and creativity, journals are best completed when you are at your most relaxed and open.

Find time during each day where you get to sit with your thoughts. Better still, to gain the maximum benefits from your journaling, find a time where you can meditate beforehand or merely take yourself out of the world. Meditating often helps you connect with yourself thoroughly before starting your journaling process.

When you feel ready and inspired, pick up the journal, do the suggested short meditation or a similar one and turn to the first prompt. Take your time to read through the suggestions and note down anything that is relevant. Sit back, take a deep breath, and let your thoughts take you on a path, writing down anything that springs to mind or enters your head as you write.

Nobody will be reading through and checking your journal. A journal, like a diary, should remain sacred. If you are to put your personal thoughts into the journal, it is imperative that you make sure it is for your eyes only. Answer the prompts as honestly as possible. Your journal is the one place where you will not be judged.

The goal of this prompts journal is to encourage you to get to the very foundations of the person you have become and digging even deeper into your authentic self. Therefore, allowing you to either make any changes that you feel are due or even congratulate yourself on who you already are.

It is not a problem if you would prefer to pick and choose your prompts for the day. Journaling is releasing, but it should also be a means of relaxing. Think of it as your much-deserved daily break. Stop everything that you are doing and sit down, claiming that time as your own. Try to resist the urge to read your journal back as you go along, as the final prompt of this book will request this as you reach the end of this journaling experience.

You owe it to yourself to be the best that you can possibly be, and more ultimately, live the life that you really want. So, without further ado, all that remains is for you to get started!

Warm-Up Exercise

As a warm-up, and in order to empty your head a bit, try to do this fast writing warm-up exercise.

Set a timer for 3 minutes and start writing. Your pen should continue to move all through the 3 minutes, and it doesn't matter what you write or draw. Jot down anything that comes to mind.

For this warm-up exercise, you can use a blank piece of paper that you can afterwards discard. If something interesting comes out of it, you can always continue with that afterwards in your journal.

Short Pre-Journaling Meditation

Meditation can thoroughly benefit your journaling process. By allocating just a few minutes per day to calm your mind and prepare your focus, you allow yourself to reap the maximum benefits on this journey of self-discovery.

Aim to do this before every journaling session:

- Set a timer, beginning with 5 minutes per day (you can increase your timer for a more concentrated and reflected course each time).

- Sit comfortably in a quiet room away from distractions.

- Close your eyes.

- Take 3 deep breaths in and then expel away your stresses with each breath out.

- Feel the different sensations in your body and listen to the sounds around you without judging or mentally commenting.

- When the timer ends, begin your journal entry for the day.

By meditating, not only do you train yourself to unlock your state of consciousness before each journaling session, but you, more importantly, ask your body to work with you to open up your mind.

"Fill your paper with the breathings of your heart"

- William Wordsworth

Day 1: The Gratitude List

Set a timer for 10 minutes. Write down a list of everything that you are grateful for, no matter how big or small it may initially seem. Set a timer and keep going for at least 10 minutes.

Let's start this journey off on the right foot and remind ourselves of the people and possessions around us that make us a very wealthy person!

the day - life. - air to breathe.
Monty
Stephen
Clare, Luke e Charlotte
My Sonna e JoAnn
Anne, Gill e Rose
Going to the gym
Hamish
The robin visiting the garden
Snowdrops - beginning to bud up.
Music I've heard today that fills my heart
Memories - Sound of Music
Lyn B.
Pauline
Food e water
the nice warm bath I've just had.
my car - being able to drive.
James - for teaching me guitar.

Day 2: Self-Rating

At the moment, on a scale from 1-10, how:

  - ❖ *honest are you:* 9
  - ❖ *intelligent are you:* 6
  - ❖ *weird are you:* 5
  - ❖ *interesting are you:* 5
  - ❖ *selfish are you:* 4
  - ❖ *present are you:* 5
  - ❖ *self-caring are you:* 4
  - ❖ *helpful are you:* 9
  - ❖ *outrageous are you:* 5
  - ❖ *funny are you:* 5
  - ❖ *crazy are you:* 5
  - ❖ *happy are you:* 7
  - ❖ *honest are you really:* 9

Which of the above results you are happy with?

Are there any of the above results you would like to change?

Comment on your discovery.

Day 3: Meeting You

Write down how you would experience meeting an identical version of yourself in another person. Describe the person and your interaction together in details.

Day 4 – Personality Test

Take the personality test at www.16personalities.com. Write about it here. Do you agree with the results and what do they make you think?

Day 5 – Roleplaying

Have a look at the different roles you play in life. Write down all of them (daughter, employee, friend, mom, patient etc.) and the characteristics of how you act in the different roles. Circle the roles you like the best, underline the ones you feel you are best at and cross out the ones you like the least.

Day 6 – The Prison Ultimatum

Spend one year in jail or marry you ex? What would you prefer and why?

Day 7 – The Dictating Letter

Write a dictating letter to everyone in your life telling them exactly how you would like them to behave and arrange themselves towards you in the future. No restrictions; on these pages you are the master everybody's behavior.

Day 8 – Making an Impression

Write down how you usually impress people. What are you actually proud of and what don't you really care about?

Day 9: That Thing That Stuck

Think of a recent event, something that happened, or you read or heard that really stuck with you. Write down how it affected you.

Day 10 – Your Clothes

Look at everything you are wearing right now. Why did you choose to put on these clothes and which purposes do they serve? What do you like and what don't you like about what you are wearing?

Day 11: – The Dating Profile

Create a dating profile promoting yourself to the best of your ability in order to attract the person of your dreams. How would you like someone to view you in writing? (It doesn't matter if you aren't single or looking for a partner, the exercise is great for self-discovery regardless).

Day 12: Choices

Every day, we make choices. Think of the hardest choice you made in the last 24 hours. What made you choose the way you did? What was essential?

Day 13: Sadness

When was the last time you were sad and what was the cause? Write in depth about how it occurred and how you coped with the sadness. Did you allow it, and did you show it?

Day 14: Response

What is your usual response and thought process when somebody praises you, pays you a compliment or is merely impressed by what you can do?

Day 15 – I Am Not

Type in "I am not" in the google search field. Pick the quote from the image results that fits you best and write it here. Why does it fit you?

_____

_____

_____

_____

_____

_____

_____

_____

_____

_____

_____

_____

_____

_____

_____

_____

_____

_____

Day 16: You Can

In order to reconsider when you catch yourself about to say, "I can't", write a list of what else you could say instead of those words.

Day 17: Changing Lives

You have been selected to trade lives with anyone for the day! Who do you choose and what are your reasons? Would you be happy returning to your own life after the day is done? Write about it.

Day 18: Your Personality Traits

List 50 positive traits you can identify with as part of your personality.

Nope, 50 is not too many!

Day 19: Other's Perception

Describe in 5 words how you think other people see you as a person. Does it match your own perception? What do others misperceive about you?

1. _____
2. _____
3. _____
4. _____
5. _____

_____
_____
_____
_____
_____
_____
_____
_____
_____
_____
_____
_____
_____
_____

Day 20 – An Intimate Question

What are the most intimate questions you would like to ask the different people in your life?

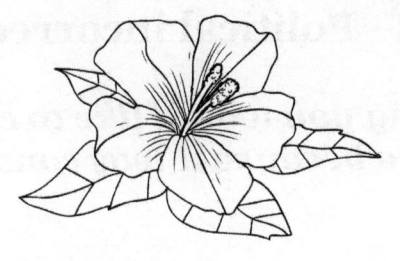

Day 21 - Political incorrectness

Write down everything you would like to express honestly that you haven't felt able to because it was considered to be politically incorrect.

Day 22: Have Fun

Write about the last time you just played the fool or laughed until you cried.

Day 23 – Outrageousness

Write down how you could be more outrageous over the course of the next month.

Day 24: Welcome Change

How have you changed during the past year? Note down how you have evolved. Include both small and big changes.

Day 25: Admiration

Name one well-known personality who you admire and respect. Choose the first that comes to mind and think about the reasons why they are your first choice.

Day 26: Achievements

List your most significant achievements to date, including educational, personal, emotional, as well as physical. Which one are you most proud of and why?

Day 27 – Better in a Year

Write down everything that is better in your life today than 12 months ago.

Day 28 – Different Outcome

Write about the times in your life that you think would have had a different outcome had you only been luckier. Write your preferred outcome.

Also, write was good about what actually happened.

Day 29: Faith

Do you have faith and is it in the form of religion, spiritual beliefs or something entirely different? Discuss this here.

Day 30: Excelling

Make a list of ten things which you think that you personally excel at and how it shows. Could you use them even more?

Day 31: Appreciating Yourself

List ten aspects that you appreciate about yourself, whether its looks, personality or something else. Explain why you choose the things that you did?

Day 32: Appreciating Your Surroundings

Take a good look around at your immediate environment. Note down all the things that you most enjoy and why.

Day 33: Make a Change

Note down what you least like about your immediate environment and work out what you could do to change it.

Day 34: Society

How do you feel about the current state of the society we live in and in which ways do you think it is better now than in the old days?

Day 35: Both Sides of a Matter

Choose a trending political debate and look at both sides of the argument. Write down the viewpoints from both sides. What is your standpoint?

Day 36: Companionship

What is an ideal companionship to you? Describe what that would be in details.

Day 37: Regret

What is your view on regrets and do you have you any reel regrets at this point?

Day 38: Organization

Would you say you are good at being organized or do you consider your lifestyle to be more spontaneous and disorganized? How does either show in your life and how well is it currently working out for you?

Day 39: Empathy

How do you approach other people that you know are having a hard time, and can you spot the signs easily in others? How would you like to approach and be approached in difficult circumstances?

Day 40: Response

"Those who suffer from depression or stress should simply pull themselves together." Write your response to this claim.

Day 41: Adulthood

Think about the way your life has been since entering adulthood. How is adulthood different from the expectations you had?

Day 42: Younger Self

With everything that you now know and have experienced, compile and write a letter to your younger self.

Day 43: Bad Habits

Name those most discerning of traits that drive you to distraction when you witness them in other people.

Day 44– Latest News

Make a google search for "Latest News". Click through to a search result you find appealing and read through it. Write out your thoughts about that topic?

Day 45 – Liking Tells

How do you know if somebody likes you? Write down all the tells.

Day 46 – Describing Others

List all the people in your life and describe each of them using only 3 words for per person.

Day 47 – Greatest Events

Write down 10 of the world's biggest events in the last decade. What are your thoughts about each event and what is your connection to them?

Day 48 – Mood Swings

Write down your beliefs and most dominant thoughts when you are in a good mood vs. when you are in a bad mood.

Day 49 – Free but Valuable

Write about something you have received that have a lot of value but didn't cost a thing.

Day 50: Fear

Okay, now you have made it to the halfway stage, congratulations! Let's move on to getting rid of those things that have been attached to you for too long.

- Write down any fears that have been crippling you for some time.
- Do not write any explanation with them, just list them.
- When this is done, write this down at the bottom of your page, "My fears are all okay, but they will not control my life any longer"

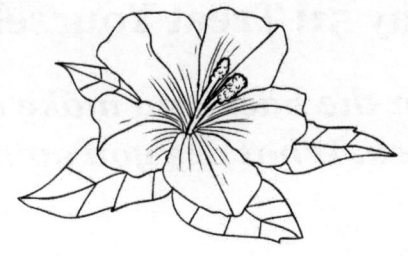

Day 51: Treat Yourself

Give yourself a pat on the back and make a written promise to treat yourself this week. What are you going to do for yourself?

Day 52 – Sharing Your Journal

How would you feel if someone else read your journal? Who would be allowed to read it and who wouldn't? What would be okay for someone else to know from your journal and what would not be okay?

Day 53 – Family Gossip

What do you think your family says about you when you are not around?

_____

_____

_____

_____

_____

_____

_____

_____

_____

_____

_____

_____

_____

_____

_____

_____

_____

_____

_____

_____

_____

Day 54 – Other's Description

Write down the names of 10 people in your life and how each of them would describe you. Who would you agree with most?

Day 55 – A Significant Impact

Write down a list of all the people who have made a significant impact on you. Then make a thorough description of all the positive features you assign to them.

Day 56 – Feeling at Home

Describe your most preferred and natural habitat. In which situations, places and company do you really thrive and feel at home? How can you tell that you thrive?

Day 57 – The Soul Mate

Describe your soul mate in detail. Include inner and outer features and characteristics, how you interact, how he or she behaves towards you and others etc.

Day 58 – Uncensored

Write down all the things you think about other people that you have always censored and never said out loud to their faces.

Day 59 – Reoccurring Thoughts

Write down those reoccurring thoughts that you haven't told anybody yet.

Day 60: Feeling Appreciated

Who makes you feel loved, cared for or special? What do they say or do to make you feel that way?

Day 61: Less Flaunting Traits

Write down a list of some of the traits which you wish you didn't have but are aware are a part of your current personality. I invite you to also write down how those traits can be view as positive traits and how they sometimes help you in your life.

Day 62: For better or Worse

Think of the people closest to you. Note down how they make you feel in different situations good or bad.

Day 63: Reaching Out

There will always be times in our lives when the going gets harsh. In those times, who are you going to call and why?

Day 64: Making Pledges

Make a written pledge to do at least one charitable act every week, whether it be within your immediate circle or further afield. Write down examples of how you can contribute.

Day 65: Returning Favors

Write down the ways which you could do something meaningful for a person you would like to treat.

Day 66: Ignorance

Though we may not be immediately aware we are doing so; can you recall a time that you turned a blind eye to something? Can you recall a time you could have turned a blind eye but didn't?

Day 67: The Real Reason

Think of the last time something went wrong between you and another person. In hindsight, what do you think was the real reason for your disagreement?

Day 68: Criticism

If you were to receive constructive criticism and learn from it, how should someone approach you?

Day 69: New Relationships

Think of a person you would like to start a friendship or a relationship with. In your best imagination, how would you like to approach this person and what would your relationship be like?

Day 70: Reconnecting

Would you consider reconnection with any past friends? With whom do you believe you could find a way?

Day 71: Making Time for Others

How much time for others would you like to make and how would you spend that time?

Day 72: Lost Touch

Think of somebody you have lost touch with but actually would like to meet again. In your own imagination, what would you like to say or write to that person?

Day 73: Dislike

Explore how you deal with those people that you really don't like or sympathize with. What did you do last time you were in the company of such a person? Would you want to do anything differently?

Day 74: Making a Difference

Write about five recent times where you made a difference for somebody else. What did you do and how did it help another person?

Day 75: Charity

If you had the chance to set up your own charity, what would you choose to support and why?

Day 76: Prevention

What do you do to prevent low energy and negative feelings taking over? List everything you could do to maintain a positive spirit.

Day 77 – Communication Means

Write down all the ways one can communicate without speaking. Then jot down how you communicate in those ways.

Day 78: Showing Emotions

How do you let people know that you care and what do you do to show your love and appreciation? Do you love conditionally or unconditionally and how can you authentically show more love?

Day 79: Morning Routine

Everyone has a morning routine consciously or unconsciously. What is your current morning routine and what would you like it to be?

Day 80: Implementing Change

List 10 daily routines such as getting dressed, brushing teeth, etc. How can you mix up your day and do something different or new? Maybe backwards? Note down what you would do and how it feels.

Day 81: Unrealistic Dreams

Create unrealistic dreams. Write down only unrealistic but intriguing visions and dreams.

Day 82: Magic Wand #1

You are given the use of a magic wand that promises only a positive outcome. What is the number one difference that you would choose to make in your life?

Day 83: Magic Wand #2

If you could use that same magic wand to change just one aspect of the outside world, what would it be?

Day 84: Acceptance

Accepting that there are some things that you can't change, list the matters that you wish could change but are just out of your control.

Day 85: Hobbies

List the hobbies that you would love to take up (again?). Are there any of these hobbies you could actively consider starting and what could be stopping you from doing this?

Day 86: The Next 24 Hours

Imagine the next 24 hours. What are you excited for and what would you rather didn't happen?

Day 87: Immediate Changes

Are there any immediate changes that spring to mind which you could perhaps employ to actively make your life better right now?

Day 88: Job Description

Describe how you feel when you are asked what you do for a living? What do you usually say? In which circumstances, if any, do you find it hard to introduce yourself?

Day 89: Elevator Speech

For the purpose of answering what you do for a living, create your unique elevator speech which you powerfully could recite in about 30 seconds.

Day 90: New Horizons

List all possible new career paths or businesses that could interests you. Don't leave any possibilities out.

Day 91: Retraining

List online or offline courses available to your individual circumstances, or educational establishments targeting adults such as yourself offering the skills you are seeking.

Day 92: Qualify

Which qualifications or skills would you like to achieve next? List everything you can think of and prioritize in the end.

Day 93: Your Book

If you were guaranteed success what kind of book would you like to publish? What genre do you immediately choose? Write down the synopsis of the book in your very own words.

Day 94: Dreamy Work

If you had the opportunity to do any work in the world for the next 30 days, what would most like to do? Make a list of desirable choices and circle your one favorite.

If you find yourself not working in any of these areas, is there a reason why?

Day 95: Life Goals

Take some time out to concentrate on what you want to achieve with the rest of your life. What do you still have left to do?

Day 96: Holding Back

Think of something holding you back in life right now that you are motivated to overcome. What would it take from you to have a breakthrough?

Day 97: In a Year

How does your life look like 12 months from now? What has changed, what are you better at, what is gone and what has entered into your life

Day 98 – Self Rating

At the moment, on a scale from 1-10, how:

- ❖ *honest are you:*
- ❖ *intelligent are you:*
- ❖ *weird are you:*
- ❖ *interesting are you:*
- ❖ *selfish are you:*
- ❖ *present are you:*
- ❖ *self-caring are you:*
- ❖ *helpful are you:*
- ❖ *outrageous are you:*
- ❖ *funny are you:*
- ❖ *crazy are you:*
- ❖ *happy are you:*
- ❖ *honest are you really:*

Which of the above results you are happy with?

Are any of the above results different from the Day 2 Self Rating?

Comment on your discovery.

Day 99 – Beginnings and Endings

Which chapters in your life are currently beginning or ending? Write a finishing statement and a proper goodbye to the chapters that are ending and thank them for everything they brought to you. Write a letter to the chapters that are about to begin and welcome them into your life.

Day 100: Congratulations!

You have completed your 100-day prompt journey! Now, take time to read and scrutinize your journal from the very beginning. What is your journal telling you about your life?

"Don't cry because it's over, smile because it happened"

- Dr. Seuss

Lightning Source UK Ltd.
Milton Keynes UK
UKHW031820141119
353548UK00008B/185/P